900

#

Maxine Lattimore JR

I L V E

Roughhouse
Breed
Ronald

It's 20 2

AFRO-AMERICANS, THEN AND NOW

by Jane Hurley
and Doris McGee Haynes

Benefic Press   Westchester, Illinois

CONTENTS

Library of Congress
Number 73-82265

Copyright 1969 by Benefic Press
All Rights Reserved
Printed in the United States of America

Unit I
Africa Beginnings

Sing a song of Africa
For children everywhere
They may not even know
That man was born there.

Birthplace of man

Long, long ago man was born. Many people today believe that man had his beginnings in Africa.

Early man did not write books so it has taken many years and hard work to learn about the past. Piece by piece men have found out about the past much as you would put together the parts of a puzzle to make a picture. What are these pieces that tell the story of early man? Bones, caves, paintings, and walls of cities help to tell the story.

As men moved to other parts of the world, they carried what they knew with them. Men came to Africa from other lands. They carried what they knew to Africa. People have always learned from other people.

Long ago kingdoms and cities

Long ago, Ethiopia was a great and strong kingdom. It was ruled by a beautiful and wise queen called the Queen of Sheba. The Ethiopians were said to be the strongest, the most just, and the most beautiful of the race of man.

Other kingdoms were built across the Sahara Desert to the west of Ethiopia. The most important of these was Ghana. Camels brought many people across the desert to Ghana. They came from Europe and Asia to trade with the people of Ghana. For gold and rubber, they traded sugar, wheat, and cloth.

Krumbi Krumbi was the most important city of Ghana. A very rich and strong king

lived there. His name was Tenkamenin. Strangers were surprised at his beautiful castle and rich clothes and crown.

Krumbi Krumbi was busy and crowded. The smell of fruits and berries filled the air, and people went about laughing and talking.

Timbuktu was another famous city in Africa. People visited this city to trade. They also came there to study at the University of Sankore. The people of Timbuktu were very proud of their schools and libraries. They enjoyed dancing, listening to music, and playing games.

Where man lived

Where man lives makes a difference. Some people of Africa made their home in the north and south where the seasons change. There it is dry in the summer and wet in the winter. It is never very cold. The Africans learned to live in the deserts, the jungles, and the grasslands, but life was very hard.

Man also learned to protect himself from some animals. Lions live in the grasslands of Africa. In the forests there are monkeys. Camels live in the deserts. Elephants live in the highlands of Africa. Because camels can go days without eating or drinking, man has used them to travel across the desert.

Africa is very rich in the gifts of nature. Many years ago, iron was used for making tools. Gold, silver, and diamonds add to Africa's many riches.

Family life

African families are very much like families everywhere. The father is the head of the house and takes care of his wife and children. In the past most Africans lived in villages. The men would hunt, fish, and take care of the cattle, sheep, and goats. They would also build the houses and protect the family from many dangers.

African women take care of the children, cook, weave, plant, and go to market. One may see a mother with a baby on her back and a basket of fruits and vegetables sitting on her head.

When they are old enough, the children help with the work, but they have much playtime. They enjoy games, riddles, songs, and dances. Every child learns about his family language and the things his people believe.

Art and music

African art is becoming well known. Benin City is famous for its wood carvings. Picasso, the great French artist, went to Africa to study carving.

African music is different from Western music. The beat is more important then the tune. The talking drums of Africa send messages and make music for dancing. From the beat of the drum, one may tell if the music is joyful, sad, or angry. Other music is made by Africans with bamboo pipes.

Folk tales

Before Africans began to write, story tellers were like books. They told the important things from the past of the people. From stories, children learn important lessons.

Some stories were told for fun. The people would join in on certain parts. Perhaps the best known of the African tales are about animals. "Br'er Rabbit" is a folk tale that was probably brought from Africa by the black slaves.

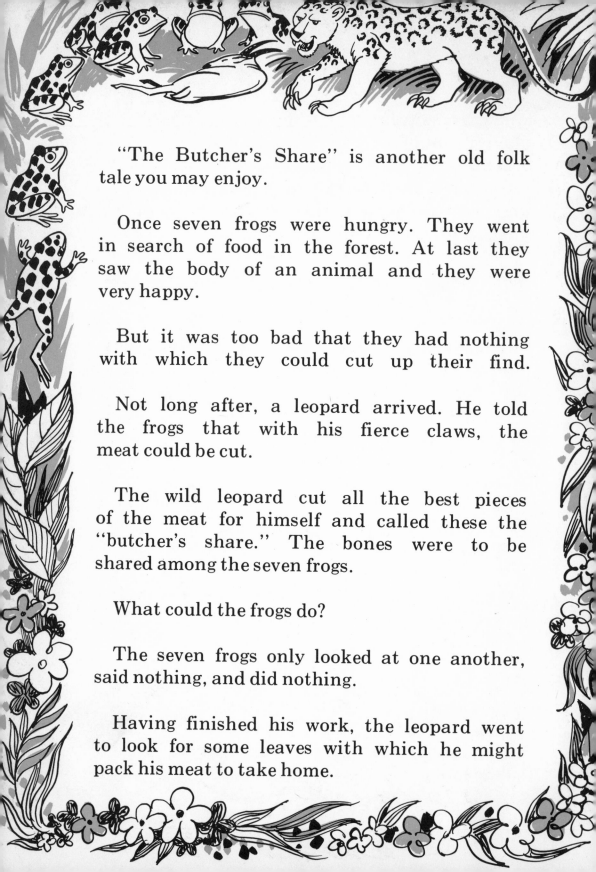

"The Butcher's Share" is another old folk tale you may enjoy.

Once seven frogs were hungry. They went in search of food in the forest. At last they saw the body of an animal and they were very happy.

But it was too bad that they had nothing with which they could cut up their find.

Not long after, a leopard arrived. He told the frogs that with his fierce claws, the meat could be cut.

The wild leopard cut all the best pieces of the meat for himself and called these the "butcher's share." The bones were to be shared among the seven frogs.

What could the frogs do?

The seven frogs only looked at one another, said nothing, and did nothing.

Having finished his work, the leopard went to look for some leaves with which he might pack his meat to take home.

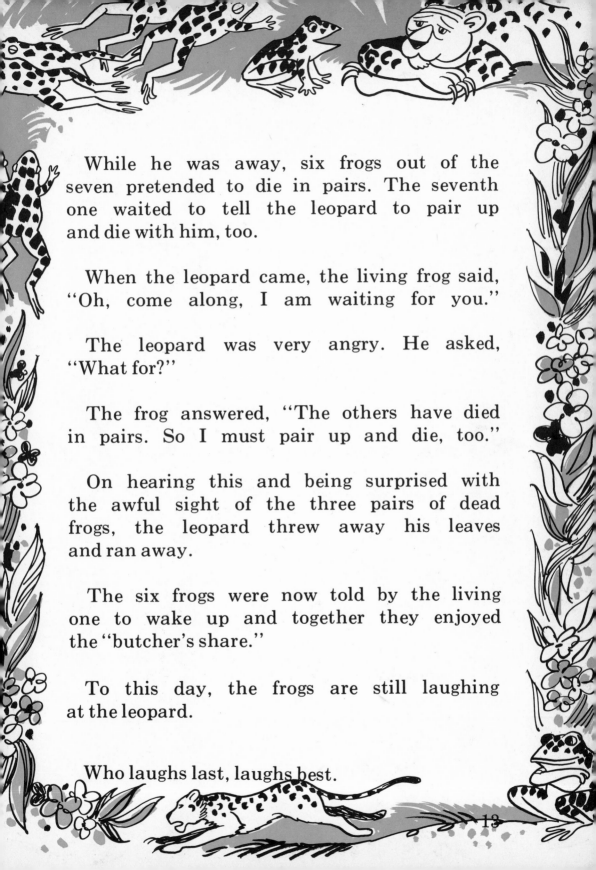

While he was away, six frogs out of the seven pretended to die in pairs. The seventh one waited to tell the leopard to pair up and die with him, too.

When the leopard came, the living frog said, "Oh, come along, I am waiting for you."

The leopard was very angry. He asked, "What for?"

The frog answered, "The others have died in pairs. So I must pair up and die, too."

On hearing this and being surprised with the awful sight of the three pairs of dead frogs, the leopard threw away his leaves and ran away.

The six frogs were now told by the living one to wake up and together they enjoyed the "butcher's share."

To this day, the frogs are still laughing at the leopard.

Who laughs last, laughs best.

New Africa

For many years, other countries have wanted the riches of Africa. Almost every inch of Africa was taken over by countries of Europe. The people were made to work for little or no money.

Battles were fought by brave African men. They felt that no one had the right to take over their land. Jomo Kenyatta, prime minister of Kenya, led his people in a long hard fight against men who took over African land. The word freedom in Kenya is "uhuru."

South of Kenya is the Union of South Africa. There the blacks are treated badly. They must live apart from the white people. *Apartheid* means held apart in South Africa.

Albert Luthuli, chief of the mighty Zulu tribe in South Africa, was a leader of his people. Like our own Dr. Martin Luther King, Jr., he received the Nobel Peace Prize for his work and care of his people. He was killed in 1968.

Africa's fight for freedom is not over. Many Africans run their country, but they do not own the businesses. Big business from countries outside Africa still run the mines and factories.

Many countries of the world are helping the Africans learn new and better ways of farming.

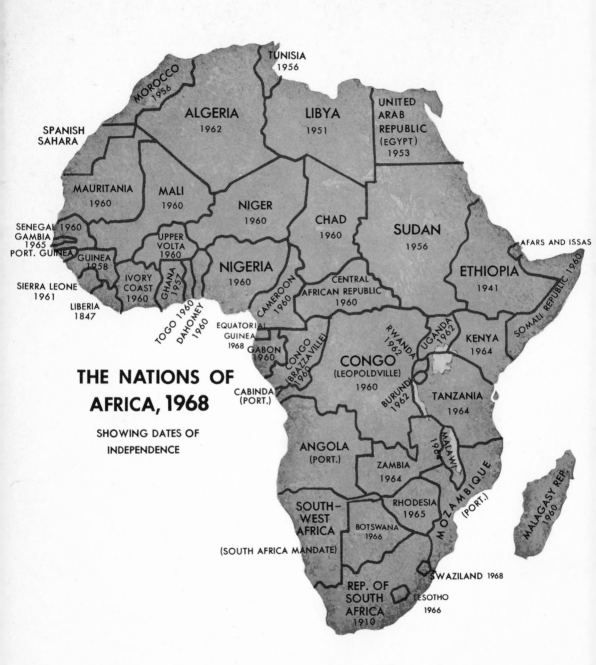

MOROCCO
1956

TUNISIA
1956

ALGERIA
1962

LIBYA
1951

UNITED
ARAB
REPUBLIC
(EGYPT)
1953

SPANISH
SAHARA

MAURITANIA
1960

MALI
1960

NIGER
1960

CHAD
1960

SUDAN
1956

AFARS AND ISSAS

SENEGAL 1960
GAMBIA
1965
PORT. GUINEA

GUINEA
1958

UPPER
VOLTA
1960

ETHIOPIA
1941

SOMALI REPUBLIC 1960

SIERRA LEONE
1961

IVORY
COAST
1960

GHANA
1957

NIGERIA
1960

CENTRAL
AFRICAN REPUBLIC
1960

LIBERIA
1847

TOGO 1960
DAHOMEY
1960

CAMEROON
1960

EQUATORIAL
GUINEA
1968

GABON
1960

CONGO
(BRAZZAVILLE)
1960

RWANDA
1962

UGANDA
1962

KENYA
1964

**THE NATIONS OF
AFRICA, 1968**

CABINDA
(PORT.)

CONGO
(LEOPOLDVILLE)
1960

BURUNDI
1962

TANZANIA
1964

SHOWING DATES OF
INDEPENDENCE

ANGOLA
(PORT.)

ZAMBIA
1964

MALAWI
1964

MOZAMBIQUE
(PORT.)

MALAGASY REP.
1960

SOUTH-
WEST
AFRICA

RHODESIA
1965

BOTSWANA
1966

(SOUTH AFRICA MANDATE)

SWAZILAND 1968

REP. OF
SOUTH
AFRICA
1910

LESOTHO
1966

16

Do these people have a feeling of negritude?

Many African young people go to Europe and come to the United States to go to school. They are learning to run their countries and their own banks and businesses.

Knowing Western ways is only one part of their learning. Most of them still speak the language of their tribe as well as one or two other languages. They also learn the folk ways of their tribes.

Negritude is a feeling of being one with black people all over the world. In America that special something is called "soul." The African word for soul is "muntu."

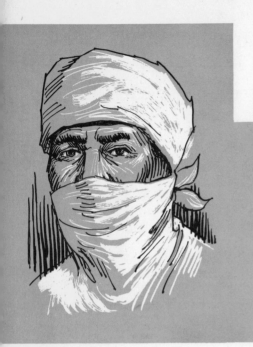

Askia Muhammed
1441-1538
King of Songhai

Once there was a wise and good king named Askia Muhammed. With the help of his friends and family he made the city of Timbuktu and the kingdom of Songhai great.

When Askia became king, there was much trouble in his country. The roads were not safe for travelers because of robbers. People were afraid to come to Timbuktu to trade. The people of the city fought among themselves. They had different ideas about gods. Some believed in one God while others believed in many gods.

18

Askia began to cure the troubles of his country by first stopping the robbers. He built a strong army to protect his people. It was said that Askia's army was so large and so fast that when they rode their horses across the desert, they looked like a "cloud of grasshoppers."

Soon all of the robbers went away and the roads were safe for travelers again. Traders came from many countries to Timbuktu. They came on camels across the deserts and they came by boat on the Niger River. They traded their goods for gold, copper, wood, and hides found at Timbuktu. Timbuktu became a rich and important city.

While some men were soldiers, others were farmers. Askia did not want his people to be lazy. His country became great because the people worked together.

At harvest time he would have his people give him some of the grain they grew. But he was not greedy. He wanted his people to have enough food for themselves. He would not let his people be hungry.

But the people still fought about gods. Askia wanted them to stop their fighting.

One day, King Askia said to his people, "I long to visit Mecca, the holy city. There I will learn much and share it with you when I return."

He took many months to prepare for his journey across the desert. A *caravan*, or train, of camels carried the gold and gifts that Askia was taking to the kings he would visit. He was welcomed by the rulers of the countries he visited and everyone was surprised with his riches.

Two years passed and his people were happy when they heard that Askia was returning. They worked hard to make his return happy. Much food was cooked for a feast, and the streets were hung with bright colorful flags.

When Askia returned, he told stories of the great and important cities he had seen. Most of all he told his people he wanted them to believe in one God as he did. Askia's own good ways set an example for his people. Many of them became Moslems.

Now that the people were not fighting among themselves, they became stronger. Askia and his army took many towns and cities to make Songhai larger. He built a road that was safe to travel across the desert to Egypt.

When Askia became old, his sons forced him to give up his throne. But he lived a long time. He lived to be ninety seven.

---

1. Why do you think Askia Muhammed was called Askia the Great?
2. What things did Askia do to make Timbuktu a great city?
3. How do you think Askia was wise?

What do these pictures show about the life of Askia Muhammed?

Some African Words to Remember

Muntu   Apartheid   uhuru

Do You Know?

1. Why is learning about early man like a puzzle?

2. How did Africans of long ago help other people?

3. How did other people help Africans?

4. What important queen lived in Ethiopia?

5. What great desert is in Africa?

6. Why did some people find it hard to live in Africa?

7. Why was Krumbi Krumbi the most important city in Ghana?

8. What is the weather like in Africa?

9. What are the riches of Africa?

10. How is African family life different from yours? How is it the same?

People and Places to Remember

Sahara	Jomo Kenyatta
Krumbi Krumbi	Ethiopia
Tenkamenin	Kenya
Timbuktu	Albert Luthuli
Benin City	Ghana

Things for Hard Workers to do

1. Draw a picture of some animals you might find in Africa.

2. Draw a map of Africa. Show the Sahara Desert, Kenya, Ethiopia, and the Union of South Africa.

3. Act out the "Butcher's Share."

4. Ask your teacher or school librarian for the "Br'er Rabbit" stories. Read one and tell the story to the class.

5. Make an African drum out of an empty oatmeal box. With tape or glue, paste the top of the oatmeal box on the box. Draw some African animals on the drum with your paints. You can make the drum "talk" by tapping it on either end with your fingers or a pencil. See if you can make the drum sound happy, sad, or angry.

Unit II
Days of Slavery

Nobody knows the trouble I've seen
Nobody knows but Jesus
Nobody knows the trouble I've seen
Oh, Glory Halleluia.

The meaning of slavery

Man has made many mistakes. In every place in the world there have been slaves. Man has often made slaves of other men.

Slaves used to do the hard work that other men did not want to do. They were made to do the work that other men did not like to do.

Slaves were bought and sold like animals or things. To be a slave meant no freedom. A slave could not say what he thought. A slave could not work at the thing he liked best. A slave could not live where he liked.

Freedom is everyone's right and people have fought wars and died for it. Today there are laws that say no one can be a slave.

Africa, homeland of the slaves

About three hundred years ago, millions of Africans were brought to America to be slaves. These people were called Negroes, or colored, because their skins were dark. Today many black people like the name African-American or Afro-American.

In Africa there were many tribes. Many times each tribe spoke a different language. This kept people apart. Some Africans sold other Africans to white men called *slave traders*. The slave traders paid for the Africans with sugar, guns, brandy, or beads. Sometimes the slave traders would catch people while they were working or walking by the sea. Families and friends never saw them again. Some Africans never reached America because they died on the crowded slave ships.

Life in a strange land

Across the ocean the slave ships carried African men, women, and children. Never would they see their homeland again with its forests, grasslands, and animals. No longer would they hear the beat of the African drum, nor the stories and songs they loved so well.

Living in a new place meant learning new ways of doing things. It meant learning a new language. There were new foods to eat. The weather was often colder than that in Africa.

When they arrived in America, they were bought by other men who had *plantations*, or large farms. Sometimes a family was sold together. Sometimes they were sold to different people. The father might be sold to one man and the mother or children sold to another. They were not thought of as people, but as animals.

At the slave auction, blacks are sold to the person who will pay the most money.

This is what a plantation was often like.

Most of the farmers in the South were too poor to buy slaves. Only one in every four farmers owned any slaves at all. Those who did have slaves usually had only a few. Most of the slaves did not have a hard life with the slave owner. But many did.

When the plantation was large, the owner needed many slaves to do the work. It was mostly on the large plantations that the slaves were treated badly.

On the large plantations, slaves lived in one-room cabins or shacks made of rough boards or logs. They had no windows, doors or floors, and little or no furniture.

28

How many jobs can you find the slaves doing?

The plantation owner or slave master lived in a big house with many doors and windows. Beautiful furniture was sometimes brought from France or England for the home. Around the big house were flower gardens, vegetable gardens, and stables for the horses. In the distance one could see the rows of cabins where the slaves lived. Beyond them were the cotton, tobacco, or rice fields where the slaves worked.

Few slave mothers cared for their own children. While the young women worked in the fields or at the big house, old women cooked and washed for the black and white children.

Many slave children never knew their fathers because they were often sold to another master. Mothers, too, were sometimes taken away from their children.

Frederick Douglass tells about the times he was so happy when his mother walked twelve miles from another plantation to see him. She would hold him in her arms and rock him to sleep. In place of his mother, Fred's grandmother cared for him along with other small children until one day when he was sold to another master.

When slave children were six or seven years old, they went to the fields to work. The boys learned to pick up trash and carry water before they learned to pick cotton.

At six or seven years of age white children went to school or learned to read or write at home. Some black children were taught to read by kind mistresses, but most slave masters thought learning to read or write would cause slaves to want to be free.

A little slave girl was taught to read and she became a famous poet. Her name was Phillis Wheatley. Frederick Douglass also learned to read and became a leader of those who were against slavery.

Slaves who worked in the fields were called *field slaves*. They got up very early in the morning and worked until night. On the large plantations, slaves planted, chopped, and picked cotton. This was very important work in the South. Great ships carried cotton up the Mississippi and Ohio rivers to factories in the North. Cotton was also shipped to other places in the world.

The owner of the plantation did not always give the orders to the slaves. Many times there was an *overseer*. This was a man who had the special job of seeing that the work was done by the slaves. He was often a cruel man who would whip the slaves if they did not work fast enough.

Work in the plantation house was done by slaves, too. They were called *house slaves*. They took care of the house, cooked, cleaned, and acted as servants. Many times they lived in the house and had a better life than the field slaves.

All men need to have fun. Because they were unhappy, the African slaves needed to laugh and sing, too. While they worked, they made up songs to make their work easier. When they were not working, they told stories or danced to forget their hard life.

Some of their songs and dances were like
the ones they had enjoyed in Africa. The
stories they told became famous folktales.
Negro spirituals, songs about God and
Heaven, are still sung today and have a very
special place in the music of America.

Slaves and Indians
Slaves who ran away from their masters
often made friends with the Indians. The
Indians did not like slavery. Some Indians had
been slaves, and they were willing to help the
black people. Hundreds of slaves became
members of Indian tribes and often married
Indians. James Beckwouth was a black, and
became chief of the Crow Indians.

Slaves fought for their freedom
When Frederick Douglass was only seven
years old, he wanted to know why some
people were slaves and others were free. Over
and over other slaves must have asked this
same question. Many ran away to the Indian
tribes. Still others ran away to the North
where they could be free. Now and then some
slaves were able to buy their freedom.

Brave men, like Gabriel Prosser and Nat
Turner, fought battles with white slave
owners to try to free their people. Many
blacks and whites died in those fights.

What does this picture show of the life of Cinque?

An exciting battle was fought at sea on a slave ship. Cinque was the handsome son of an African chief who was taken into slavery. On the way to America, he took command of the ship and tried to take it back to Africa. He failed and the navy captured the ship. The ship was returned with the slaves to America. Cinque and his shipmates were put in prison, but later won their case before the United States Supreme Court. They were returned to Africa.

The Underground Railroad used many ways to help the slaves escape from the South.

Abolitionists

Many people believed that slavery in America was a terrible mistake. They set to work to free the slaves. They were called *abolitionists*. They wanted to *abolish*, or stop, slavery. They wanted laws made that would forbid slavery.

William Lloyd Garrison, a white abolitionist, wrote stories in his newspaper of how bad slavery was. He traveled to many cities making speeches against slavery.

Frederick Douglass, Sojourner Truth, and Harriet Tubman were important black people who worked to free slaves. They made many trips to plantations in the South and helped slaves to freedom by way of the *Underground Railroad.* The Underground Railroad was a number of secret trails over which black slaves traveled to freedom in the North and Canada. Some of the slaves walked the trails at night, hiding in the woods or in the barns and houses of friendly people during the day. Other slaves were hidden in wagons and driven over the trails by friendly people.

Thousands of Afro-American men, women, and children found freedom through the Underground Railroad. Black and white people helped them.

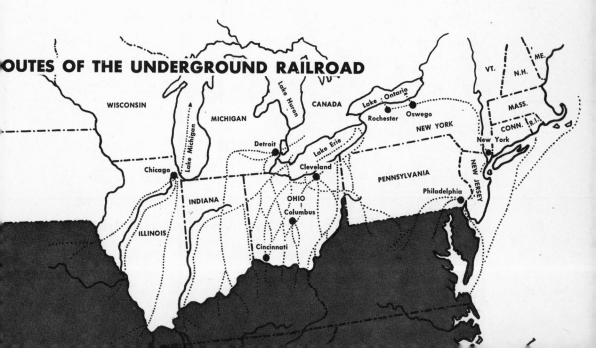

ROUTES OF THE UNDERGROUND RAILROAD

Benjamin Banneker
1731-1806
Mathematician

The lights were going out in the farm houses near Baltimore, Maryland. People were going to bed. But one young man was just waking up. Soon he would be out in the fields. Benjamin Banneker's "day" was beginning. He was not going out into the night to farm. Ben would spend the night watching the stars.

When the other farmers started their day, Benjamin would be going to bed. His father's farm was not a joy to Ben. He did not like farming. Benjamin Banneker would rather spend his time learning.

As a boy, Ben had enjoyed going to school more than working on the farm. At school he could learn. There were so many things to study about. Ben was a good pupil. He made very high marks.

Mostly, Ben liked to learn things about science and machines. When he was about twenty years old he made a wooden clock. The clock would chime the hours and kept perfect time for the rest of Ben's life.

When his father died, Ben had to take over the farm. He could no longer spend his time learning things.

Benjamin's friends, the Ellicott family, knew about his need to learn. They bought the farm from Ben. So that he would have a place to live, the Ellicotts let Ben stay on the farm. Each year they paid Ben a part of the cost of the farm.

The Ellicotts gave Ben books to read. He read about the stars. He studied about numbers. He learned to measure the land. Ben studied so well that he was soon able to show the Ellicotts mistakes in the books.

Because of all that he had learned, Benjamin was able to tell what the weather was going to be. Farmers would come to him to find out the best time to plant their crops.

At the age of sixty one, Benjamin wrote an *almanac*. An almanac is a book that tells about the weather, gives ideas for better farming, and tells the movement of the stars.

George Washington, the first President of the United States, was planning to build a capital city. He had chosen a Frenchman, Pierre L'Enfant to build the new city. A group of Americans were chosen to help L'Enfant. Benjamin Banneker was part of this group.

Before the city was finished L'Enfant and President Washington got mad at each other. L'Enfant took the plans for the new capital city back to France. Benjamin was the only one of the group who had helped L'Enfant and could remember the plans. He remembered them so well, he was able to draw them. The city of Washington, D.C. would not be the beautiful city it is today if Benjamin had not had such a good memory.

Benjamin was very unhappy about slavery in America. He wrote a letter to Thomas Jefferson. In his letter, he told Mr. Jefferson it did not seem right for America to fight a war to be free from England and not let the black man be free, too.

Benjamin could not end slavery. But he was able to show people that a black was able to learn things and use what he had learned.

---

1. How did Benjamin feel about learning? Do you feel this way? Why?
2. What do you think the farmers thought about Ben watching the stars?
3. How did Ben use what he learned?

What do these pictures show about the life of Benjamin Banneker?

Paul Cuffe
1759-1817
Ship Captain

"Heave to!" shouted the captain of the British ship. "Heave to or we'll blow you out of the water."

The American whaling ship followed the order and moved to the side of the British ship. The sailors on the American ship were taken prisoner. They were taken to New York and put in prison. Sixteen year old Paul Cuffe was one of the sailors.

The Americans and British were at war. Paul was kept in prison for three months. When he was let go, the war was still going on. Paul decided to stay on a farm near New York until the war was over.

After the war, Paul began a sailing business with a small open boat. Paul loved the sea. While he had stayed on the farm, Paul taught himself about sailing. He studied and learned to sail a ship on the open sea.

In his sailing business, Paul carried goods from town to town along the coast from New Bedford, Massachusetts. Many times he was caught by pirates. They would take his goods and destroy his boat. But Paul would not give up. Each time he built another boat and started out again.

His sailing business grew and grew. People in the cities where his ship stopped could not believe a black man was a ship captain.

In Massachusetts, blacks were not allowed to *vote*. They could not choose the people who made the rules and laws for the state. Only whites who owned land or houses could vote. Paul and his brother John went to the courts. They told the court that they owned land and should be able to vote. The state of Massachusetts passed a new law in 1783 which said that black men could vote, too.

Paul had not been able to go to school when he was a child. He had to teach himself all that he knew. When his children were ready for school, Paul saw to it that they had a school to go to. He used his own money to build a school house on his own land. He found a teacher for the school. Then Paul gave the school to the town so that other black children could go to school.

Paul was not a slave. He had never been one. But Paul cared about the black people who were slaves. When a slave could buy his freedom, he had no place to go. Paul became interested in a place where blacks who were free could go to live. In 1811, Paul visited Sierra Leone in Africa. This seemed just the place for the free blacks to make a new start. Back in America, Paul talked to many people to get their help in taking the blacks to Sierre Leone. In 1815, Paul returned to Africa with thirty-eight blacks.

He planned to take many more people to Sierra Leone to live, but he became sick and died before he could do so.

Paul Cuffe's father had been a slave. He bought his freedom. Paul left $20,000, farm land and houses, and a good sailing business when he died. Most important, he left good will for blacks among the whites of New Bedford, Massachusetts.

---

1. What three things did Paul Cuffe do to help the black man?
2. Is it important for people to vote? Why?
3. Why do you think Paul would not give up when pirates kept taking his goods and destroying his boats?

What do these pictures show about the life of Paul Cuffe?

Phillis Wheatley
1753-1784
Poet

The eyes of the little black girl were wide with fear. All around her were people and loud voices. The voice of the man who pulled her to the slave block was loudest of all.

"What will you give?" he called out.

John Wheatley and his wife heard the noise, too. They were walking along the Boston street.

"John, they are selling that little girl as a slave," said Susannah Wheatley. "We must help her."

John Wheatley pushed up to the front.

He called out. The little black girl was sold to him at once.

At the Wheatley home the eight year old little girl saw one thing that looked like her African home. She ran into the garden and put her arms around the flowers. She smiled and cried at the same time. She had been in the dark slave ship for three months. Now she knew that she was safe.

The Wheatleys named her Phillis meaning "green branch" because of her love of flowers. They gave her their last name.

Mrs. Wheatley began to teach Phillis just as she had her own two children. Phillis learned all the things that a young lady of Boston should know.

Soon Phillis began to write poems. She found she could make sad times less sad and happy times more happy by writing about them. Her first poem was printed when she was sixteen.

Phillis was not strong, and the Wheatleys thought she needed a trip. When Phillis was twenty, they sent her to England with their son Nathaniel. Here Phillis wrote more poems. Soon most of London knew her.

A book of her poems was printed in England in 1773. She was the first American Negro to have a book of poems printed.

Then bad news came. Mrs. Wheatley was ill. Phillis was free. She could do as she wanted. She loved the people who had been so good to her. Phillis took the first ship home.

Soon after Phillis got to Boston, Mrs. Wheatley died. It was a sad time for Phillis. Mrs. Wheatley had been like a mother to her.

After a time, Phillis became the wife of John Peters, in the garden of the Wheatley home. Phillis left the home she loved so much.

Phillis wrote poems that helped the people of Boston. It was a time of war and her words gave the people hope. Phillis became known as the poet of the American Revolution.

Phillis did not get much money for her poems. One by one the Wheatleys had died. There was no one to help Phillis, John, and their three children. The family became poor and ill. Phillis died on December 5, 1784.

Phillis left a beautiful gift for all Americans. One of her best poems, "Liberty and Peace" was printed after she died.

1. Why do you think Phillis liked the Wheatley garden?
2. What are the three things that the Wheatleys did to help Phillis? How did Phillis help others? Why was it hard for Phillis to leave London when she did? Read what tells you why Phillis went home.
3. How did Phillis help herself? Why is it good to learn to help yourself? In what ways can you help yourself?

What do these pictures show about the life of Phillis Wheatley?

Jean Baptiste Pointe Du Sable
1745-1818
First Settler of Chicago

The bear skin over the door moved. A tall strong looking Indian came into the room. He was followed by other Indians. They were covered with war paint. Jean Baptiste Pointe Du Sable was frightened for himself and his three friends. He tried to think of something that might save them.

Most of the Indians of the Illinois country were friends of the French. Du Sable took a chance. "I am a Frenchman and friend of the Indian," he said in French. "My three friends are friends of the Indians, also."

The tall Indian smiled. "I am Pontiac, chief of the Ottawa Indians," he said, "and we are friends of the French."

Chief Pontiac ordered Du Sable and his friends set free. And so began a friendship that was to last until Pontiac died.

Jean Baptiste Pointe Du Sable was born on the island of Haiti. His father was a Frenchman and his mother a freed slave. Du Sable had come to America to buy furs from the Indians.

Soon after their meeting, Pontiac was shot by an Indian who pretended to be his friend. Before he died, Pontiac asked Du Sable to speak to all of the Indian tribes and tell them not to go to war over his death.

Du Sable began to travel the Illinois country speaking to the tribes for Pontiac. During a visit to the Potawatomi tribe, Du Sable met a beautiful Indian girl named Kittihawa, Fleet of Foot. He wanted to marry her. He could not marry her unless he was a Potawatomi. It was not easy to become an Indian. There were many hard tests but, Du Sable passed the tests and became a Potawatomi Indian in 1771.

While traveling through the Illinois country for Pontiac, Du Sable had seen a beautiful place called *Eschikagou* by the Indians. He thought it would be a fine place for a trading post. In 1772, he built a cabin there near Lake Michigan.

Du Sable brought his wife and members of the Potawatomi tribe to live in Eschikagou. They were the first family to stay in what is now the city of Chicago.

The Indians planted gardens and Du Sable built up the trading post. Now, all who passed going from St. Louis to Detroit and Canada had a warm fire, hot food, and a place to rest on their journey. The Du Sable Trading Post was the best between St. Louis and Montreal, Canada.

The new country of the United States began to send settlers into the area. Du Sable was a man who loved the wild country and settlers meant neighbors. He did not like the changes that were coming to his Eschikagou.

Du Sable sold his trading post in 1800 and moved to Saint Charles, Missouri. There he spent his last years telling people what it was like in Eschikagou. He died in 1818. The Indians always said that the first "white" man in Eschikagou was a black man.

---

1. What good did Du Sable do by opening his trading post?
2. Why do you think Pontiac did not want the Indians to go to war over his death?
3. What did the Indians mean when they said the first "white" man to settle Eschikagou was a black man?

What do these pictures show about the life of Jean Baptiste Pointe Du Sable?

Frederick Douglass
1817-1895
Speaker and Writer

"Stop? Don't you know there will be trouble because of what you are doing?"

"What are we doing that is wrong?" asked Mrs. Auld. She looked down at Frederick Augustus Washington Bailey. He held the book close and tried not to show his fear.

"Fred is black," said Mr. Auld. "He is our slave. Maryland says you cannot teach a slave to read or write."

Mrs. Auld did not know about this. She had to stop teaching Frederick to read, but this didn't stop him from learning.

He read everything he could find. The boys on his Baltimore, Maryland street became his teachers. He knew he had to learn to read, write, and talk well to become a freeman.

Mr. Auld let Fred work for a ship builder. At first Fred could keep some of what he earned. Later Mr. Auld took all the money Fred got for his work.

As he worked for the ship builder, Fred made friends with a man. He helped the man get work. Soon the man gave Fred some papers. The papers would help Fred travel without being stopped.

Many times Frederick was in danger. By the time he got to Massachusetts, his money was gone. But, he was free.

Fred changed his name to Frederick Douglass. No one was looking for a slave with that name.

Fred began to think about the other slaves who were not free. He went from place to place telling about his days as a slave.

Frederick was a good speaker. In 1845, he wrote a book about his life. When Mr. Auld read *The Narrative of the Life and Times of Frederick Douglass*, he wanted Fred back.

Fred had to move fast. He went to Boston and sailed for England. His ship had just left when men came to take him back to Mr. Auld.

Frederick stayed in England two years. He went from place to place talking about slaves. Frederick made many friends. They raised the money to buy Frederick from Mr. Auld. They gave Frederick money to start his own paper.

Frederick went back to America and started *The North Star*. He called his paper this because runaway slaves followed the north star at night. *The North Star* told black people what was happening in America.

Later a war began. President Lincoln called Frederick Douglass to Washington, D.C. Frederick wanted President Lincoln to let black men fight in the war. Lincoln said yes. Frederick's sons Charles and Lewis went into war at once. Almost 200,000 black men went into the war.

The war ended, and the slaves were free. Frederick Douglass went on working for the rights of black men until he died. He came from slavery to speak to the world for his people. Frederick Douglass was a great American.

---

1. Who helped Frederick Douglass become free? Did Frederick help others? Who? Tell about people you help or who help you.
2. Why did Frederick Douglass face danger when he wrote a book about his life as a slave? What does this tell you about him?
3. Why did Frederick Douglass go on with his work after the war?

What do these pictures show about the life of Frederick Douglass?

Harriet Ross Tubman
1826-1913
Underground
Railway Conductor

"Harriet! Harriet!" someone said softly.
Harriet turned from her work to the other
slave who was nearby. She listened carefully.

"They are going to sell you, Harriet," the
slave said. "I heard them talking about it."

Harriet did not say a word. She ran quickly
to get her blanket. It was the only pretty
thing that was really hers. Then Harriet ran
into the woods.

A white woman had said she would help
Harriet if she needed it. Now was the time
to find out if it was true.

The white woman opened the door at once when Harriet came to the house. She told Harriet that she was part of the "Underground Railway." This group of people helped slaves get to freedom.

The woman gave Harriet something to eat and told her how to get to the next place where she could find help. Harriet thanked the woman again and again. Then she gave the woman her blanket. It was the only way she could show how much finding a friend did for her.

When night came, Harriet went into the woods. Long ago her father had showed her how to walk through the woods with no sound. He taught her the wood plants that were safe to eat. Now Harriet knew why.

At the next place a farm family helped her. When night came, the farmer put Harriet in his wagon. All night he drove until they came to the river. Here another man took her up the river.

For many days and nights Harriet was helped by many kind people. She hid in piles of hay, in holes, and in houses. At last she came to Philadelphia and freedom.

Harriet soon found that it was not enough

to be safe but alone. She wanted to help her family and others to be free. Harriet worked hard for money to help.

Once again Harriet went through the "Underground Railway" to bring her sister and her family to safety. Harriet Tubman made nineteen trips back to Maryland to bring slaves to freedom. She became a wanted woman. At one time there was $60,000 for the one who caught her.

Each trip was dangerous. Pictures of Harriet were everywhere. One time some men saw Harriet. They thought of the picture. Quickly Harriet picked up a newspaper. Her quick thinking saved her. The men knew that Harriet Tubman could not read. This woman could not be the one. The men went away.

Harriet gave a sigh. She had been afraid that she was holding the paper upside down.

In the ten years that Harriet brought slaves to freedom, she helped 300 black people. When the days of slavery were over, Harriet went to live in New York. The people of the New York town where she lived are proud of Harriet Tubman. Here they honor her and tell about what she did. She is thought of when people tell about the lives of brave people who helped build the United States.

---

1. How had her father helped her get ready for her trip through the woods? How do your family or friends help you get ready for when you grow up?
2. Did Harriet know all the people who helped her? Was it easy? Why?
3. Why did Harriet go back to Maryland? Do you think she was brave? Why?

What do these pictures show about the life of Harriet Tubman?

Words To Remember

plantations   field slaves
overseer   abolitionists
slave traders   Negro spirituals
house slaves   Underground Railroad

Do You Know?

1. What were some of the things a slave could not do?

2. What name is liked better by many black people?

3. Why did some slave children never know their parents?

4. Why were the blacks and Indians friends?

5. What was it like to be a slave in a strange land?

6. Why did slaves sing and dance?

7. What was the job of the overseer? How did he do his job?

8. Do people work better when they enjoy their work? Why?

People To Remember

Cinque

Phillis Wheatley

Frederick Douglass

James Beckwouth

Nat Turner

Gabriel Prosser

Sojourner Truth

Harriet Tubman

William Lloyd Garrison

Things for Hard Workers To Do

1. Act out the story of Cinque. Show how he took control of the slave ship. Act out his talking to the judges of the high court.

2. Make a play about slave days. Choose people from the class to be slaves, slave traders, plantation owners, sellers of slaves, and overseers. Be sure your play tells how the slaves were caught, carried to America, and sold. Remember to tell about the different kinds of work the slaves did, where they lived, and how they acted. Give each person in your class a part in the play, then present the play for another class or for your parents so they may learn about slave days, also.

3. Look in the library for books about the Underground Railroad. Find out about other people who helped with the railroad besides Harriet Tubman. Make a map of the route of the railroad for the class bulletin board.

Unit III
Freedom For All

Free at last
Free at last
Thank God Almighty
I'm free at last!

The Civil War

A hundred years ago, America was young. There were only thirty-one states that could be reached by river boats. There were few trains and stage coaches. The Pony Express carried mail across the prairies to the West. It took weeks and sometimes months for people and news to travel. There were a few big cities like New York, Philadelphia, Boston, Baltimore, and Cincinnati. People from all over the world came to America. They brought their beliefs, customs, and ideas with them and settled in many places all over the country.

When our country began, it was said that in order to last the people would have to work together. America would be one nation, with liberty and justice for all. But there was not liberty and justice for all. Black men were kept as slaves in the South.

Most of the people of the North worked in factories. Most of the people of the South had farms. The different ways of life kept them from understanding each other. When laws were made for the country, each group tried to make the laws best for them.

Each time a new state was added to the country, the problems between the North and South were argued in Congress. Each part of the country wanted the new state to follow their ways.

For a time, Congress tried to keep things even by letting a southern state and a northern state join the Union at the same time. Each time, though, the fights in Congress became worse and worse.

The South kept slaves. The North did not. The South said they needed the slaves to pick the cotton on the large farms. They said the slave was treated better than the factory worker of the North. The North wanted the South to stop keeping slaves. Each time a new state was added, the North tried to keep slavery out of the new state. The South said that each new state should decide for itself about slavery.

Finally, the arguments grew so bad that the South said it could not belong to the country anymore. The South said it would be a new country called the *Confederate States of America*. And so the Civil War began.

It was a very bad war. Sometimes fathers fought sons, and brothers fought brothers. Cities and farms of the South were burned. Battles were fought on land and sea.

When the Union, or northern soldiers marched through the South, slaves ran away. They hid in the swamps and the hills. Some went North and joined the northern army.

Many black soldiers fought on the side of the Union. One brave black sailor, Joachim Pease, was given the Navy Medal of Honor for the brave things he did in a sea battle.

Side by side, white women and black women worked in the camps and hospitals. They cared for the soldiers and gave medicine to the sick and wounded.

Emancipation Proclamation

In 1863, President Abraham Lincoln was troubled. Americans were killing Americans. He had said, "We cannot be half slave and half free. This is like a house divided against itself."

President Lincoln had written a paper which said that all the slaves were free. But he did not know whether to sign it or not.

Frederick Douglass was the big voice saying to Mr. Lincoln, "Free the slaves, free the slaves. Let my people go."

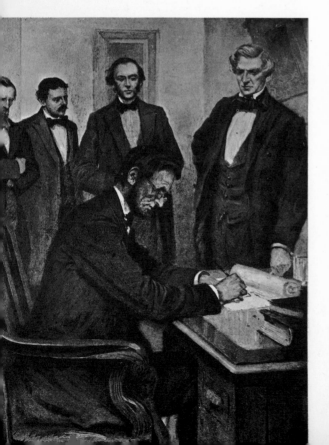

President Abraham Lincoln signs the paper that gave the slaves freedom. Watching him are members of the President's Cabinet. The Cabinet members are those people who help the President decide what is best for the country.

One day President Lincoln signed the Emancipation Proclamation. Black people will always remember that day. The paper said the slaves were free. Some people shouted, some cried, some sang and danced.

After the long time of slavery, the black man was free. Now fathers and mothers could find their children and make a home for them. Friends could be together again.

Reconstruction

After the Civil War ended in 1865, there was much work to be done. The country had lost thousands of men. The cities, farms, and factories of the South had been burned. For two hundred years the black people had been slaves. Now they were free, but many did not have jobs, homes, clothing, or food. Because they had not gone to school, many could not find jobs.

Some black people stayed on the plantations. They had no other homes to go to. They worked as *sharecroppers* for the plantation owner. This meant they would farm the land and give part of their crops to the owner. They lived in the same slave cabins and worked for ten or fifteen dollars a month. But now the owner was no longer giving them food or clothing. They had to grow their food, and buy their clothing from the small pay.

Some of the white people of the South thought the black man should still act like a slave. They treated him badly. It was necessary for the government to keep soldiers in the South to protect the freedmen, as the free slaves were called after the war.

Many people from the North came to the South to help the people build again after the war. A special board was set up to help the black man. It was called the *Freedman's Bureau*. It helped to raise money to build homes, churches, schools, and hospitals. Many white women came from the North to teach black children in the schools.

Proud black people from Africa would now begin a new life in a land no longer strange. They would become teachers, doctors, lawyers, scientists, writers, and statesmen.

For ten years after the Civil War, black people did have important jobs in the South. Robert Wood became the mayor of Natchez, Mississippi. Pinckney Pinchback was the governor of Louisiana. Some black men even helped to make the laws for the country. Robert Smalls was in the House of Representatives. Blanche Bruce became a Senator. In South Carolina, more black people were elected to public office than whites.

The southern people were afraid that the black people would take their land and government. Some of these southern people tried to frighten the black man out of holding public office. They would dress in a white sheet with a hood over their heads and come to the black's home in the night. When the black people would not leave, their homes, churches, and schools were burned. Some were beaten and killed.

The southern states that had been a part of the Confederate States of America could not belong to the country right away after the war. The United States said they would have to have certain laws first. When the South made these new laws and seemed not to need the help of the Union soldiers any more, Reconstruction came to an end.

Hiram Revels is being sworn in as Senator.

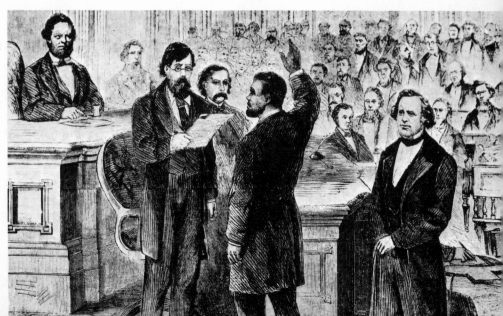

WHITE   **COLORED**

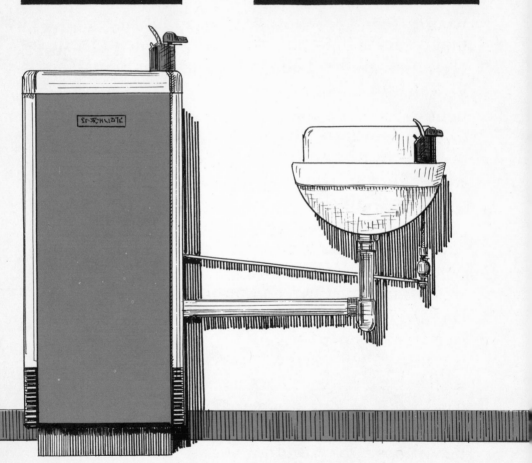

Segregation

Now that the northern soldiers were no longer needed in the South, the southern states began to make laws which said the black people were to be kept apart from white people. The law makers promised that the blacks would have the same things as the whites, but they would not be together. This was *segregation*. The black people were separate at school, at church, and in their neighborhoods. Black people could not eat in a white restaurant. They could not drink from the same water fountain. Black people had to sit or stand in the back of buses and trains even when there were empty seats in the front. In public places there were signs which read; "For whites only," or "For colored."

Black people would never be slaves again. But under the new laws they would always be reminded that they did not have the same rights as the whites. The only reason seemed to be their color. Their color kept them out of good schools, out of good houses and neighborhoods. Their color kept them out of good jobs. For almost one hundred years, the black people lived in the South under the laws of segregation.

Many black people went North where they would have more rights. They looked for better homes, jobs, and schools for their children.

Afro-Americans vote for the people who make the rules and laws of our country.

Life in the cities

Thousands of the black people moved to the cities of the North, the East, and the West. They worked beside white people to build the highways, bridges, and railroads of the country. They became bus drivers, policemen, firemen, plumbers, and mechanics. More black people went to college.

Since Reconstruction Days many black people could not vote in the South, so they did not make the laws. When they moved to the North, they used their vote to help choose several black people for public office.

When there were only a few black people in the cities in the North, East, and West, there were not so many problems. As millions moved out of the South, the northern schools and neighborhoods became crowded.

When some black people moved into white neighborhoods, their homes were bombed. They found the same hardships in the cities that they had left in the South.

William DuBois started the *National Association for the Advancement of Colored People* in 1909. This is a group of people much like the Freedman's Bureau. It helped black people when they left the farms and moved into the cities. Among the many things the NAACP did was to help black people get voting rights in the South. It helped them fight segregation in the schools and in the public places.

The *Urban League*, which started in 1910, helped newcomers find jobs and homes in good neighborhoods in the cities. It helped find ways to relieve the crowded conditions.

Oscar DePriest, Adam Clayton Powell, and William Dawson were among the first northern men elected to Congress. They helped make the laws that gave black men more rights.

Matthew Henson
1866-1955
Explorer

Matthew Henson looked into his friend's face and was proud. Robert Peary had just given him a very great honor.

"You're asking me to go to the North Pole with you," said Matt. "Think of it! We'll be on top of the world together."

Robert Peary laughed. "Not so fast, Matt," he said. "We have a long way to go before we get there. That's why I need good men to go with me."

Matthew Henson nodded. He had been on many trips with Robert Peary. It seemed a long time since the young officer had come in the store where Matt worked.

He told of a trip he was taking and said he needed a good man. The shop owner told Perry about Matt. Before he knew it Matt was with Robert Peary in Central America.

Wherever they went, Peary and Matt were friends. They shared many dangerous and exciting adventures together.

Matt heard a lot about Peary's dream of reaching the North Pole. Now Peary was asking him to go on the greatest adventure of all. It was a trip to make a dream come true.

Peary, Matt Henson, and other men had tried to get to the pole before. They had always had to turn back. Could they make it this time?

"We'll have to get through this time, Matt," said Peary. "I won't be able to make the trip again. It's this time or never."

There were hard days ahead for Matthew Henson and Peary. But hard days had been a part of many of the trips they had taken.

They used sleds pulled by dogs to travel across the ice and snow. But the ice and snow were over water. Soon they came to a place where there was water. There was no land.

When the water froze the men were on their way again. Mile after mile slipped away as the sleds moved. Peary stopped often to take readings of where they were.

"Only 60 miles to the pole," said Peary. "We must make it, Matt."

"We will," said Matt. He told the Eskimos with them to move out again. They did what Matt asked at once. Matt's dark skin made him seem like them.

On and on they went. At last Peary stopped to take another reading. "We're here Matt," he said. "We made it to the pole."

Peary gave Henson the flag of the United States. "Here is the flag, Matt," he said. "You put it up."

Matthew Henson put up the flag. A strong Arctic wind pulled at it, but the flag stayed in place. It was a dream come true for Peary and Henson.

Many honors were given to Henson for his work with Peary. People all over the world wanted to meet him. For Henson the greatest honor had come when Peary first asked an unknown black man to go with him to the North Pole.

1. Why did Matthew Henson give up his work to go with Robert Peary to South America? Was the work Henson did with Peary easy? What do you do to help your friends?

2. Had Peary and Henson tried to get to the North Pole before? Read the part that tells about it. What does this tell you about Henson and Peary? Did they give up easily?

3. What was the highest honor that Peary gave Henson? Why was this an honor? Why did Peary want Henson with him?

What do these pictures show about the life of Matthew Henson?

Bill Pickett
1860-1932
Cowboy

The horse ran beside the running steer. The young man on the horse's back got ready to jump. The horse was close beside the steer. Bill Pickett jumped to the steer's back and reached for its horns. He grabbed the horns in his hands and slowly began to make the steer turn its head. When the steer's nose came up, Bill grabbed the steer's lip in his strong teeth and pulled. The steer fell to the ground. Up went Bill's hands to show the crowd he was not holding the steer down. Bill had bulldogged the steer.

A cheer went up from the crowd. Some of the people stood on their feet and clapped. Some of the people could not believe what they had seen. Bill had thrown the steer without the help of his horse or a rope. Other cowboys would always rope the steer first then pull it down with the help of their horse.

Sometimes cattle on the ranch would get themselves into places that a man or horse could not go because the brush would be too thick. The ranch dogs would go in and bark at the steer to get him moving. When this didn't work, the dog would jump and bite the lip of the steer and pull him out. This was called bulldogging.

The Miller 101 Ranch, near Bliss, Oklahoma was not just a cattle ranch. The ranch also put on a show called a rodeo. This was a show where all the cowboys could show the things they did every day in their work. They had races in riding bucking horses, steer riding, and roping calves.

Bill Pickett was the first to bring the sport of bulldogging to the rodeos. He had learned to bulldog cattle on the 101 Ranch. He got the idea from the ranch dogs.

From 1905 until World War I, the 101 Ranch put on rodeos. Sometimes they were held at the ranch. Sometimes they were held during the Frontier Days in Cheyenne, Wyoming.

People came from all over to the Frontier Days show. The streets of Cheyenne were crowded with happy people. When the rodeo began, every seat was taken. All of the people were waiting to see Bill Pickett.

The Miller 101 Rodeo traveled all over the world. They gave their show in Madison Square Garden in New York. They gave their show in Chicago; London, England; and Mexico. The greatest thing that happened to Bill Pickett was performing his bulldogging for the King and Queen of England.

After World War I, people lost interest in the rodeos, and the show no longer traveled around the country. Bill Pickett stayed on the Miller Ranch. He was needed by the Miller family to help work the ranch.

One day when he was working with a horse, Bill was thrown and kicked by the horse. When the other men on the ranch found Bill he was badly hurt. Eleven days later he died of the wounds from the kick of the horse.

Bill Pickett brought a new kind of show to the rodeo. He was the first to wrestle a full grown steer to the ground. He gave the rodeo bulldogging.

1. Does a cowboy need to be brave to bull-dog a steer? Why?
2. Why is it hard to do something the first time before anyone tries it?
3. Where do you think you might be able to see a rodeo today?

What do these pictures show about the life of Bill Pickett?

Daniel Hale Williams
1856-1931
Physician and Surgeon

Daniel Hale Williams

James Cornish lay bleeding from the chest. He had been hurt with a knife in a street fight. The knife had cut close to his heart.

When he was brought to Provident Hospital, the doctors said there was nothing they could do. No one had ever operated near the heart before. They could not save James' life.

"Well, I'm going to try to save him," said Doctor Daniel Williams.

Doctor Dan, as he was called by friends, found doctors willing to help him. They wheeled James Cornish into the operating room.

Doctor Dan opened James chest. He quickly sewed up the cut near the heart and closed the chest. James Cornish was still alive. Doctor Dan had done the operation everyone said could not be done. But would James live?

Two months later, James Cornish left the hospital a healthy man. Doctor Dan had saved him without the help of modern medicine. The operation had been done without the help of X-ray, blood plasma, or modern operating equipment. The world had none of these things in 1893. Doctor Dan had only the will to try to save James Cornish.

When Doctor Daniel Williams began as a doctor, there were no hospitals in Chicago where a black doctor could work. With the help of friends, Doctor Dan started the Provident Hospital in Chicago in 1891. Along with the hospital he began a nurses training school for black nurses. Here, black girls who wanted to be nurses could come and study.

President Cleveland heard about Doctor Dan. He asked him to come to Washington, D.C. and be the head of the Freedman's Hospital. This was a hospital for black people.

Again, Doctor Dan started a school for

black nurses. He also opened the hospital as a training center for black doctors.

When other doctors heard of the operation Doctor Dan had done on James Cornish, they wanted to see him operate. Doctors from all over the country came to the Freedman's Hospital to watch Doctor Dan operate.

In 1913, Doctor Dan was given a great honor. He was made a charter member of the American College of Surgeons. This means that Doctor Dan was invited to be among the first doctors to start the American College of Surgeons.

Doctor Dan returned to Chicago and went to work at Saint Luke's Hospital. He was the first black doctor to perform an operation at Saint Luke's.

While at Saint Luke's, Doctor Dan held a clinic in surgery each year. Doctors came from all over the country to study at Doctor Dan's clinic. They learned new ways of doing things in the hospital. They learned new things that would make operations safer and easier for the sick people. Many of the things done in surgery today were first done at Doctor Dan's clinic.

Doctor Daniel Williams saw the needs of his

people and went to work to fill the needs. Even after his death he continued to help his people. In his will he left one half of his estate to be used to help black doctors.

1. What do you think was the most important event in Doctor Dan's life? Why?
2. How did Doctor Dan help his people? Did he help white people, too? Tell how.
3. Was the operation on James easy to do? Why? Is it an easy operation today? Why?

What do these pictures show about the life of Daniel Williams?

Ethel Waters
1900-
Actress

The young woman sat at the dressing table. She was thinking about how she came to be in this dressing room in the Empire Theater. It seemed a long time ago that she had worked as a house maid. Now, here she was, the star of a play on Broadway.

She thought of all the great actresses that had used this room. Many were dead, but many would see her on the stage tonight. Would they like her? Would the play be a success?

Ethel was acting the part of a very sad mother in the play. As she acted, Ethel remembered the sad life of her grandmother. The people watching her knew she was doing more than acting a part. She was living the part.

When the play was over the people clapped and clapped. They called Ethel back to the stage seventeen times. People said she was the finest living actress of the time, black or white.

Ethel Waters was now the highest paid woman in show business. She had come a long way from being a maid for $4.75 a week.

When Ethel was seventeen she got a job as a singer. She planned to sing for two weeks and then go back to her job as a maid in Philadelphia.

Wanting to sing something special, Ethel wrote to W.C. Handy, asking him if she could sing his famous song, "The Saint Louis Blues." Mr. Handy said yes, and Ethel became the first paid singer to sing "Saint Louis Blues."

Ethel never went back to her job as a maid. People enjoyed her clear, beautiful voice. It made people happy to listen to her sing. She sang in bigger and nicer clubs.

At first Ethel was not called by her real name on stage. They called her "Sweet Mama Stringbean." When it was said that "Sweet

Mama Stringbean" would be singing, the club or theater would overflow with people.

Other singers would come to hear her sing. It was so much fun listening to her sing that sometimes the clubs would stay open as long as Ethel would sing. Sometimes she and the people would sing together all night.

Other people who could not come to the clubs wanted to hear Ethel sing. The Columbia Record Company made records of her best songs. She was thought of as the best black singer.

Miss Waters first love was acting. Her first real chance to act came when she was chosen to be in the play "Mambo's Daughters."

After seeing her act, people knew that Ethel Waters was as great an actress as she was a singer. From then on she went up and up in show business. By 1935, she had come from a $4.75 a week maid to a $4,000 a week actress.

Ethel Waters is an important singer and actress. She has played on the stage in New York, in movies in Hollywood, and sometimes can now be seen on television.

She has always believed God helps those who help themselves and so she has worked hard at everything she has done. Before she goes on the stage Ethel Waters says a prayer for God's help. After each performance, she thanks God for His help.

---

1. Have you ever had a part in a play? Was it easy to act? How did Ethel Waters feel about acting?
2. Have you ever seen Ethel Waters on television? Tell about it.
3. Why do you think she was called "Sweet Mama Stringbean?"

What do these pictures show about the life of Ethel Waters?

W. C. Handy
1873-1958
Composer

"Take that guitar out of this house! That guitar is sinful! Take it back to the store and buy a dictionary. A book will do you more good than music," said Mr. Handy.

The boy's face fell. He had worked hard all year selling fruit, nuts, and soap. He had saved his money for so long. William Handy wanted to learn to play the guitar. But his father thought all music except singing was wrong.

W. C., as everyone called William Handy, took the guitar back to the store. But he never gave up wanting to learn about music.

Music time at school was W. C.'s happiest time. His teacher taught W.C. all that he knew about music. He taught him about the different kinds of music.

When he was eighteen, W. C. decided to try to earn his living with music. He left home and traveled with the Lauzetta Quartet. They sang in clubs and churches from Florence, Alabama to Chicago, Illinois.

From Chicago, they sang their way to St. Louis, Missouri. In St. Louis, W. C. decided he could not make enough money to live on with music, so he left the Lauzetta Quartet.

It was not easy. Not everyone wanted to hire a black. The jobs he did get did not always pay very much money. Many of the jobs he took only because they kept him near music. One of his jobs was as a sweeper in a music hall in Kentucky.

W. C. got a job with the Mahara's Colored Minstrels as a cornetist in 1896. Things began to look better for him. He was a real musician now.

One night when he was playing with Mahara's band he began to remember the hard times he had. As he played, his music began to show the sadness he felt. The people enjoyed this sad music. They called it "blues" because of the sad sound.

W. C. often thought about the hard times he had in St. Louis, and he wrote a song about it. It was called the "St. Louis Blues." The first line of the song is about the law that blacks could not be on the streets after sundown. "I hate to see that evening sun go down, I hate to see that evening sun go down," are the first words of the "St. Louis Blues."

W. C. knew that many people enjoyed listening to sad music. He and a friend opened the Pace and Handy Music Company in Memphis, Tennessee. Many famous blues songs were written by W. C. and sold by the company. But the "St. Louis Blues" was always the best.

Blues songs were not the only things W. C. wrote. He wrote important symphony pieces, too. The "Aframerican Hymn," and "Blue Destiny," are two of his best.

He once told a group of children, "Life is like this trumphet, if you don't put anything in it, you don't get anything out of it."

Many people in America and all over the world have enjoyed Mr. Handy's music.

There are schools, parks, and theaters named after W. C. Handy, but his best memorial will always be the "St. Louis Blues."

---

1. How did blues music get its name? Do you think there is a better name for sad songs? What name would you give sad songs?
2. Do you agree with W. C.'s father about music? Why?
3. What did Mr. Handy mean when he told the children life was like a trumpet?

What do these pictures show about the life of W.C. Handy?

Words To Remember

Sharecroppers   Segregation
Reconstruction   Freedman's Bureau
NAACP   Urban League

Emancipation Proclamation
Confederate States of America

Do You Know?

1. Who was President at the time of the Civil War?

2. Why did he say that America was like a house divided?

3. What great black man told the President to free the slaves ?

4. What was the Emancipation Proclamation?

5. What was Reconstruction?

6. What important jobs did black people have during Reconstruction?

7. Where did black people go when their rights were taken away in the South?

8. When black people got a good education, what were some jobs they did?

People To Remember

Abraham Lincoln   Blanche Bruce
Robert Wood   William Dubois
Pinckney Pinchback   Oscar DePriest
Robert Smalls   William Dawson

Adam Clayton Powell

Things for Hard Workers to Do

1. Go to the library and find books about famous black people. Tell the class about them and what they are famous for.

2. Draw a map of the United States for your class bulletin board. On the map put the names of the cities where these famous black people live. Put the names of these Afro-Americans on the map. See if you can find pictures of them and add these to the map. If you cannot find a picture of the person, draw a picture of what they are famous for and put this on the map.

3. Make a play about the Emancipation Proclamation. Be sure the play tells how President Lincoln felt about slavery. Have someone play the part of Frederick Douglass. Get books about Douglass and Lincoln from the library to help you.

Unit IV
Today's Leaders

We shall overcome,
We shall overcome,
We shall overcome someday,
Deep in my heart,
I do believe,
We shall overcome someday.

Finding out about Afro-Americans
of yesterday and today

Many people do not know what Afro-Americans have done because too often books, papers, magazines, and television did not tell about them. Therefore, much of what Afro-Americans have done in the past is new and exciting today. Many black heroes like cowboys, explorers, inventors, thinkers, and soldiers have not been known.

When people go to the city of Boston, they may see the statue of the first American to die in the Revolutionary War. His name was Crispus Attucks. Like many other black men, he died for his country a long time ago.

Thousands of black soldiers fought and died in the Civil War. Many more went around the world in ships, airplanes, and submarines in World Wars I and II and helped to keep our country free. Benjamin O. Davis, Sr. became the first black general, and his son was made a general, also.

Black explorers helped to build our country. Estevanico, called Little Stephen, was one of the first to settle the state of Arizona. Jean Baptiste Pointe Du Sable built the first trading post on Lake Michigan where Chicago now stands. He is called the first citizen of Chicago, Illinois.

On a visit to Washington, D.C. one can see the work of a black man who lived many years ago. His name was Benjamin Banneker. He helped to plan the beautiful streets in the city where our President lives.

Dr. George Washington Carver was a great Afro-American scientist. He made over one hundred products from the peanut, soy beans, sweet potato, and clay. He worked at the Tuskeegee Institute where many black students still go to college.

Dr. Daniel Williams operated on a man's heart in the Provident Hospital in Chicago in 1893. It was the first time a person had lived after this kind of operation.

Another famous black doctor is remembered for starting the blood bank at the time of World War II. He was Dr. Charles Drew.

Dr. Theodore Lawless helps people with skin diseases at his clinic in Chicago. People come to him from all over the world.

Afro-Americans brought their gift of making music from Africa. Black singers and dancers have entertained kings and queens. Many say that Marian Anderson is America's greatest singer. She was invited to sing for the Metropolitan Opera.

W. C. Handy has been called the father of the blues. He wrote "St. Louis Blues." Since his time other blues and jazz artists have become famous. You have probably heard records made by Dizzy Gilespie, Ray Charles, Louis Armstrong, and Duke Ellington. Mahalia Jackson is a great gospel singer. Leontyne Price and Dorothy Maynor are concert artists and opera stars. Sidney Poitier is a famous movie star who was the first black artist to win an Oscar award. You may know other famous black artists from seeing them on television and in the movies.

These people are Sidney Poitier, Gwendolyn Brooks, Jackie Robinson, and Carl Stokes.

In 1945, Jackie Robinson was the first Afro-American invited to play on a major league baseball team. Before 1945, Afro-Americans had to play on the Negro Baseball League. Willie Mays now plays baseball with the San Francisco Giants. He is thought by many to be the greatest all-around player in baseball history.

Other famous black athletes are Jack Johnson, Joe Louis, Sugar Ray Robinson, and Muhammed Ali, who were great prize fighters.

Six Afro-Americans sit in Congress and help make our laws. They are Congressmen William L. Dawson, from Chicago; Adam Clayton Powell, from New York; Charles Diggs, Jr., from Detroit; Robert Nix, from Philadelphia;

Can you name the people pictured above?

Augustus Hawkins, from Los Angeles; and John L. Conyers, from Detroit.

Edward Brooke was the first black to be elected attorney general of a state. He is now a Senator from Massachusetts. There are two black mayors of important cities. They are Carl Stokes of Cleveland, Ohio and Robert Hatcher of Gary, Indiana.

Afro-Americans have been outstanding writers since the time of Frederick Douglass. Paul Lawrence Dunbar wrote many poems that sounded like the spirituals the slaves sang. Langston Hughes wrote many poems and books for boys and girls. Gwendolyn Brooks is a great poet who lives in Chicago, Illinois.

The struggle for civil rights

For Afro-Americans, the struggle for civil rights has been long and hard. More than one hundred years ago the freed slaves sang "Free at last." Black people are still fighting for freedom. Even when the laws change, some people do not want to treat Afro-Americans like other Americans.

In 1955, a black woman named Mrs. Rosa Parks, would not give her seat to a white man on a bus in Montgomey, Alabama. She said she was tired. When she was taken to jail, black people became very angry. Dr. Martin

Because Mrs. Rosa Parks was tired, these blacks no longer have to ride in the back of the buses.

Luther King, Jr. was pastor of the Dexter Avenue Baptist Church in Montgomery. When he was told about Mrs. Parks, he remembered the time he was put off a bus in Atlanta, Georgia. He was in high school, and his teacher was on the bus, too. When he and his friends became angry, she asked them not to cause trouble. He thought, "Now we will do something about this."

Many people met at his church and decided not to ride the buses until the law was changed. This was the beginning of the Montgomery Bus Boycott. Old people walked, children walked, mothers carried their babies and walked. One woman said she was walking so her children and grandchildren would be free. Dr. King and many of his friends were beaten and put in jail. But the people still walked. After a year, the law was changed and black people did not sit in the back of the bus any more.

Dr. King died fighting for civil rights. He was in Memphis, Tennessee helping the garbage men when he was shot. He gave his life to help poor black and white people. His dream that every American is important will not die. Afro-Americans are Americans, too. Their rich gifts, like the gifts of other Americans, make America great. Everyone is important and, like a family, everyone must work together.

Benjamin Davis, Jr.
1912-
Air Force General

The young man worked hard over the papers in front of him. All around him other young men were working, too.

The same thought went through his head again and again. "Will I pass? Will I pass?"

Once before the young Afro-American had tried to get into West Point. It was very hard. Most of his answers to the questions had to be right. The time before he did not have enough right answers to pass.

Benjamin Davis wanted to pass as much as he had ever wanted to do anything.

Very few Afro-Americans had ever finished West Point. Benjamin wanted to add another name to the list of men who had.

Benjamin Davis was bright. He hoped that he was bright enough to pass. Congressman DePriest had given Benjamin two tries at West Point. This time he must make it.

Soon Benjamin had the happy news. This time he passed. He could go into West Point.

Benjamin's father was a colonel. Ben had lived at different places all his life. His father went from place to place doing his work.

The Colonel was very proud to have Benjamin go into West Point. He was prouder still the day Benjamin's West Point days were over. Benjamin Davis, Jr. became an officer.

At that time an Afro-American had to go into an Afro-American group or teach at an Afro-American school. Benjamin Davis went to teach in an Afro-American school.

Benjamin did well. When a flying school was opened he learned to fly. He won his wings. By 1943 he was a colonel teaching other men to fly. The United States was at war. Soon Benjamin Davis led his men in the work of the air war.

The men of the United States were ready. An air strike was planned to help make the surprise landing from ships work well.

Benjamin Davis and his men were ready. Their air strike was of help to the men who made the landing from ships.

As the war went on Colonel Davis and his men went out again and again. The brave men won honor after honor. Colonel Davis was very happy the day that his father came to honor a brave man. General Davis was proud of his son as he gave the Flying Cross to Colonel Davis.

The brave Afro-Americans of the 332nd Fighter group did well. After the war, President Truman said that Afro-Americans should not be put only in groups of other Afro-Americans. He said that they should be able to be in any group. Benjamin Davis had to work hard to bring this about. He won here just as he had in the war.

In 1965 Benjamin Davis became the first Afro-American Lieutenant General of the Air Force. General Davis now does his work in Washington, D.C. He has brought honor to his country and his people.

Benjamin Davis did not give up his work. He went to war again for his country. His work took him all over the world.

---

1. Did Benjamin Davis give up? Read something that tells about this.
2. Do you think Benjamin was proud of his father? Why is it good for a son to be proud of his father?
3. What right did President Truman give Afro-Americans after the war? Why?

What do these pictures show about the life of Benjamin Oliver Davis, Jr.?

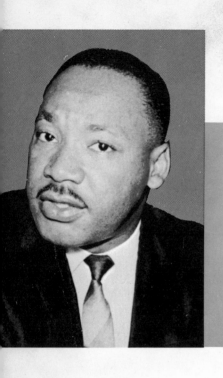

Martin Luther King, Jr.
1929-1968
Minister

The young man stood at the front of the church and leaned forward to talk to the people.

"I am asking you to walk," he said. "Walk if there is no other way. It is better to walk with freedom than ride without it."

Martin Luther King, Jr. quickly told the story of Rosa Parks. She had been tired from a day's work. When she got on the bus, she sat in the first seat she found. The bus became crowded and the bus driver told her to go to the back of the bus.

Rosa Parks said, "No."

Now Martin Luther King asked the black people of Montgomery, Alabama to say "no" with Rosa Parks. He asked them to say "no" to a Montgomery rule that said black people must ride in the back of buses. He asked the people not to ride the buses again until the rule was changed.

The people listened to what Martin Luther King had to say. For 381 days they rode in cars or wagons or walked.

There was no trouble. No one was hurt. But nearly 17,000 black people did not ride the buses of Montgomery.

Martin Luther King was put in jail for telling the black people not to ride the buses. There was a rule against forming a group of people to keep business from a company.

Martin Luther King's case was sent from one court to another. At last it went to the Supreme Court of the United States. This is the high court of the United States.

The Supreme Court said the rule was not good. The rule had to be changed. Martin Luther King had acted in peace, and he had won. Rosa Parks and the other black people of Montgomery could ride the buses of Montgomery again. They could sit on any seat on the bus that was not being used just as anyone could do. They could ride in freedom.

Dr. King helped form the Southern Christian Leadership Conference. It was to help black people all over the United States. Dr. King helped form this group just as he had formed the group in Montgomery to help the black people there. Dr. King went wherever his help was needed. He went to cities in the north and in the south. He went to other parts of the world telling about his work and what he believed.

Honor after honor was given to Dr. King as he went from place to place. He led black people in many peaceful freedom marches. In 1964 he was given a very great honor when he received the Nobel Peace Prize in Oslo, Norway.

Dr. King was shot in 1968. He was doing the work to which he had given his life. His words and his dream of a world where black people and white people can live together in peace goes on. The dream of Martin Luther King, Jr. lives on in the hearts of people everywhere.

1. Why did Martin Luther King ask the people of Montgomery to walk? Do you think this was a hard thing for the people to do? Why? Do you think he was right? Why?
2. Why didn't Martin Luther King stop his work when the rule about black people riding in the back of buses was changed? Would you have stopped when this happened?
3. Did the killing of Dr. King end his dream? What was his dream? What will you do to help the dream come true?

What do these pictures show about the life of Martin Luther King, Jr.?

Althea Gibson
1927-
Tennis Player

"Swat! Swat!" The tennis ball hit the wall hard and bounced back. The young girl swung again.

It seemed funny to see Althea Gibson hitting the ball again and again with no one to send it back, but no one laughed. Althea was able to take care of herself. No one laughed at her.

Althea was very good at playing many games. She won at everything she played. Althea worked very hard to win when she played a game.

"I think you can play tennis," a friend had said. "I think you should try the game."

Now Althea was trying to learn to hit the ball hard and make it go to the place she wanted. This was not as easy as it seemed.

There were no tennis clubs in Harlem where Althea lived. Althea had to work by herself much of the time. She wanted to know what she was doing and do it well before she went to the tennis clubs uptown.

After a time Althea began to play with other players. At first she lost. She had to learn how to lose well. In Harlem she never gave up. She won because she wouldn't say that she had lost.

Althea did not have to be a good loser many times. Soon she began to win tennis games. She did well enough that she was asked to play tennis for the United States in other countries. She won games in many countries.

Then she went to England to play at Wimbledon. These games were thought to be the most important of each year. Here Althea lost.

Althea made up her mind that she would go back to Wimbledon. She had to win. In 1957 she went to the Wimbledon games again. This time she won. Queen Elizabeth honored her as the winner.

When she went back to New York, the whole town seemed to come out to meet her. She rode in a parade through the city. The city gave a dinner in her honor. It was an exciting day for the girl from Harlem.

There was another set of games Althea wanted to win. These games were the most important to her because the winner was judged to be the best tennis player in the United States. The day came when Althea Gibson was the winner at Forest Hills, New York. Vice-President Nixon honored her as the best woman tennis player in the United States. This honor was the best of all.

Althea Gibson went back to Wimbledon. She won again. To win at Wimbledon once could be luck. To win two times showed she was the best at her game. This was an important honor for her and for the United States.

Tennis games took Althea Gibson all over the world. She was a winner again and again in one country after another. In each place she went she left good will for America and good will for all the people of her race. The girl from Harlem now belonged to the United States and to the world.

1. Why do you think people might have laughed when they saw Althea Gibson hitting the ball in the park? Why did no one laugh?
2. Is it possible to always win at anything? Why? Why did Althea Gibson have to learn to be a good loser? How can you show that you are a good loser as well as a good winner? Which is harder? Why?
3. Why was winning the United States games so important to Althea Gibson?

What do these pictures show about the life of Althea Gibson?

Percy Julian
1899-
Chemist

The two men stood quietly watching the two small glass dishes. In each dish were some grains of something that looked like sand. Under each dish was a flame. The men were hoping the grains in the two dishes would melt at the same time.

Dr. Percy Julian had worked for three long years trying to find a way to make a medicine to help people who could not see well. There was a medicine for this, but it came from a special plant and cost a lot of money. If Dr. Julian could learn how to make the medicine from chemicals, it would help many people and cost only pennies. If the grains from the plant melted at the same time as those Dr. Julian had made then they would know Dr. Julian had been able to make the medicine. All of the work Dr. Julian had done would not be wasted. The grains melted at the same time. Dr. Percy Julian had found the way to make the medicine. Now many people could be helped for very little money.

Professor Blanchard wanted Dr. Julian to be the head of DePauw University, but other people at the school did not believe that a black could do the job. Dr. Julian left the University.

Just at this time the Glidden Company asked Dr. Julian to come to work for them. The Glidden Company wanted to see how many things could be made from the soybean. They needed the best chemist to do the work. Dr. Julian was the best chemist.

While he worked for the Glidden Company, Dr. Julian made many things that have saved lives and helped people. He made a foam that puts out fires. He made many medicines that help people have easier and happier lives.

When he was a small child, Dr. Julian's father wanted nothing but the best from his son. He made Percy be the best in every thing he did. As he grew up, Percy tried to do as his father asked.

Dr. Julian graduated from the DePauw University in Greencastle, Indiana. He graduated with the highest marks and was given the honor of being named to the Phi Betta Kappa. At Harvard University, he earned a master's degree in chemistry. Percy Julian wanted to learn all that he could about chemistry. With the help of a friend, he went to Europe to study at the University of Vienna. Here he became a doctor of chemistry.

Dr. Julian left the Glidden Company after a while and opened the Julian Laboratory in Franklin Park, Illinois. Here many wonderful medicines have been made by Dr. Julian that have helped people.

Dr. Julian is the grandson of a slave. His father was a railroad clerk. It is a long hard way from the slave cabins of a plantation to one of the best chemists in the world.

Dr. Julian lives in Oak Park, Illinois. He spends all of his spare time in his garden.

When spring comes each year, Dr. Julian's yard is full of flowers. It has been called the "house of a thousand tulips."

---

1. Dr. Julian worked a long time finding the medicine for people's eyes. Why do you think good things take a long time to do?
2. Dr. Julian's grandfather was a slave. How important do you think school is?
3. What did Dr. Julian's father expect of him? What do your parents expect of you?

What do these pictures show about the life of Percy Julian?

John H. Johnson
1918-
Publisher

The young man sat on the edge of his chair. He had told his story before. Always the answer was the same. John Johnson had an idea. It was a good one. But it was hard to get anyone to listen to him. He was trying once more. This time he was at the office of a company that could lend money.

John Johnson had a part-time job while at Northwestern and Chicago Universities. Here he came upon an idea. In his work he had to read many magazines to find stories about black people like himself.

John found stories, but he had to look in many magazines. Most Afro-Americans did not have time to read many magazines. They could read only a few.

Once more John Johnson told his idea to the men in the company office."Don't you see the need?" he asked. "Black people need their own magazine. I need money to start it. I'll call it 'Black Digest.' I will have stories about black people."

The men at the company office looked away. John Johnson thought he had lost again.

At last one man turned to him. "I'll tell you what, Mr. Johnson. We'll give you $500.00. That's all we'll give."

John Johnson smiled. "It's not much," he said. "But it's a start. I'll take it."

The $500.00 sent out the first 5,000 "Negro Digest" magazines. John Johnson and his wife worked on the magazine at night. He had another job during the day.

The magazine did well. The 5,000 magazines were sold before the first week was past. More magazines were sold each month.

When "Negro Digest" did well, John Johnson knew he was right. There was a real need for magazines about black people and their life. He had an idea for a picture and news magazine for black people. There was not enough paper for the new magazine during World War II. In 1945, the first copies of "Ebony" were printed.

"Ebony" did very well. John Johnson added two other magazines. "Tan" is a magazine for women, and "Jet" is a pocket size news magazine with some pictures. Each magazine answers a real need of black people.

As the magazines have grown, John Johnson has become famous. His name is known far from his home in Chicago, Illinois. In 1951, he was named one of America's Ten Outstanding Men of the Year by the United States Junior Chamber of Commerce. He was the first black man to be given this honor.

John Johnson is known throughout the United States and in other parts of the world. Presidents Eisenhower, Kennedy, and Johnson have asked him to visit other countries for the United States.

Today Mr. Johnson has an important part in many businesses. He works with the boards of several schools. Above all John Johnson works to keep a dream alive. He believes that by knowing each other better people can learn to work together. He works each day to make that dream come true.

---

1. What help did John Johnson need to start Negro Digest?

2. Why did Johnson's magazines do well? What other things can you think of that did well for the same reason?

3. What was Johnson's dream? What is your dream?

What do these pictures show about the life of John H. Johnson?

Whitney Young, Jr.
1921-
Civil Rights Leader

The young man read the letter in his hands again and again. "Come to Atlanta," it said. Whitney Young was asked to be Dean of Social Work at Atlanta University.

Whitney knew what his answer must be. He liked Omaha. He liked his work with the Urban League here. But he had always worked in the North. The black people of the South needed help. Whitney knew he should take this job in the South to help his people. He put down the letter. He must go where the need was great.

Whitney Young believed in hard work. His bright mind and hard work had brought him through Kentucky State College in 1940. Now he went to work at Atlanta University. Soon what he did began to show. The school went ahead with his help. Young people from Atlanta went out to help others all over the United States.

Since 1947 Whitney Young had worked for the Urban League. After a time he was asked to leave Atlanta and go to New York as head of the Urban League. It was hard to leave Atlanta. He had done well. He had many friends. He wanted to stay, but he knew he could do the most good as head of the Urban League. Whitney Young went to New York.

The Urban League began to change quickly after Young came. He worked for better schools for black children. Black Americans had a lot to give. Whitney Young wanted them to help make a better America.

When Time Magazine picked twenty-five of the finest Americans to go on a trip to Eastern Europe, Whitney Young was among them. He made many friends on this trip.

Some of the men asked him to take jobs for much money. But again Whitney Young knew the answer. His place was with the Urban League.

One man on the trip remembered Whitney Young. Henry Ford, II, was a rich man. He had talked with Young about the Urban League. He knew they needed money. Soon after the trip Whitney Young received a check for $100,000 from Mr. Ford.

Whitney Young had told the story of the Urban League well as he had many times before. He went on with his work. Many times he received honors for the work he did.

Whitney Young went on with his trips. He told his story wherever he went. He told all America of the needs of black Americans. He told what the Urban League did and wanted to do to help the black people.

Some people wanted Whitney Young to leave the Urban League and find a better place for himself in the world. But as always Whitney Young did not stop. He had a job to do. Whitney Young would not stop his work until the troubles of black Americans were ended for all time.

1. Why did Whitney Young go to Atlanta? Why did he go to New York? Why was it hard for him to leave each place?
2. What places did Whitney Young live? Would you want to live in many places? Why? Is going to a new place always better?
3. What was Whitney Young trying to do? Did he do a good job? Read your answer from the book. What can you do to help?

What do these pictures show about the life of Whitney Young?

Edward Brooke, III
1919-
United States Senator

The election was over. Edward Brooke and his friends sat waiting for the votes to be counted.

"You'll win, Ed," said a friend. "You've worked too hard this time to lose again."

"Losing three times is not easy." said Mr. Brooke. "I just can't lose a fourth time."

The telephone rang. Brooke's friend answered and then began to cheer. Brooke had won the election. Edward Brooke was the new Attorney General for the state of Massachusetts. He was the first black man to be elected to this high office in any state in the United States.

Edward Brooke thought about all the other elections he had been in. He had lost three times. Each time had taught him a little more about how to win. Each time he had met more people and made friends with them. And now he had won a very important office in his state.

He wanted to be a very good Attorney General. He worked hard at the job. When it was again time for the people to choose a man for the job, Mr. Brooke was elected again.

Edward Brooke did such a good job as Attorney General that when he decided to run for the office of United States Senator, many people voted for him.

Edward Brooke has been given many honors. He was named one of the ten most outstanding men in Greater Boston. He was given the Spingern Medal by the National Association for the Advancement of Colored People. He has been given the Charles Evans Hughes Award for brave leadership in government service from the National Conference of Christians and Jews. But the greatest honor he has received has been the people of his state wanting him to be their Senator.

During the time he was trying to be elected to his first public office, Edward Brooke was appointed by the Governor of Massachusetts to the job of Chairman of the Boston Finance Committee. This was a job where he was to watch the spending of government money. While he held this job, he uncovered many places where the government's money was not being used as it should be. Many people who were not honest were found out by Mr. Brooke. Because of this he made many people happy. They knew that he was seeing to it that their money was not being wasted.

When he became Attorney General, he stopped the wasting of money in that office.

Mr. Brooke has never worked for civil rights in the way most Afro-Americans have. He has not marched or taken part in sit-ins. But he has worked for civil rights by always doing the best job he could.

He has turned down many jobs because he thought they were being given to him because of his color. He has always believed that a man should be chosen for a job because of what he can do, not because of his color. Mr. Brooke has said, "Only then do you have progress."

---

1. Is it important to have honest people in government jobs? Why?
2. What are civil rights? What difference do civil rights make in your life?
3. Does the color of your skin, or hair, or eyes help you do a better job at school? Why?

What do these pictures show about the life of Edward Brooke?

Gwendolyn Brooks
1917-
Poet

A large number of people filled the school library. All the chairs in the room were filled. Many of the people stood. The room was still. It seemed as if all the people at the Chicago school wanted to get into the library at one time.

Everyone listened as Gwendolyn Brooks read her poetry. Important guests and young people were held by the wonder of the words of the soft-voiced black housewife.

She ended her reading with her poem, "Tommy" from *Bronzeville Boys and Girls.*

Gwendolyn Brooks read, "I put a seed into the ground and said, "I'll watch it grow.'

I watered it and cared for it as well as I could know.

One day I walked in my back yard and oh, what did I see!

My seed had popped itself right out, without consulting me." *

No one moved. For a minute there was no sound. Then everyone began to clap.

Gwendolyn Brooks was happy. She had given the black young people something to keep them trying. She made the important guests wonder if they had done enough to help. She had brought a feeling of warmth to everyone in the room.

Gwendolyn Brooks felt at home with the Chicago people. Though she started life in Topeka, Kansas, Chicago had been her home for many years.

It seemed as if she had written poems all her life. Her first poem was written before she was seven years old.

When she was a young girl, her friends wondered why she stayed home while they went to parties.

*Bronzeville Boys and Girls

Copyright © 1956 by Gwendolyn Brooks Blakely
by permission of Harper and Row, Publishers

People didn't understand even though one of her poems was in print by the time she was 13.

Gwendolyn Brooks lived in a second floor flat on a corner. She could look out into the streets. She wrote about what she saw and heard. Her poetry told about the every day life of black people in the city.

Her first book brought her many new readers. The name Gwendolyn Brooks was heard in Chicago and throughout Illinois.

Prize after prize was given her. She was named one of ten outstanding women of the year in 1945. In 1946 and 1947 Gwendolyn Brooks received a Guggenheim Fellowship. This money was to be used to live while writing new poems. She could hardly believe all that happened to her.

In 1950 she received the prize of prizes. She received the Pulitzer Prize for Poetry for her poem *Annie Allen*.

One poem followed another and more prizes came her way. She wrote a book, *Maud Martha*. In 1968 Gwendolyn Brooks was named Poet Laureate of Illinois.

Miss Brooks still talks of herself as a housewife, mother, and part time poet. The part time poet has given full time to her family, her people, her Illinois, and her America.

---

1. What words does Gwendolyn Brooks use to tell about herself? What does this show about her?
2. What does Gwendolyn Brooks write about? What would you write about?
3. Why did Gwendolyn Brooks read her poetry to others? How do you think this might help?

What do these pictures show about the life of Gwendolyn Brooks?

Words to Remember

Montgomery Bus Boycott

Do You Know?

1. Why didn't people know very much about Afro-Americans?

2. What famous statue of an Afro-American is in the city of Boston, Massachusetts?

3. What did Estavenico and Jean Baptiste Pointe Du Sable do?

4. What teacher at Tuskeegee Institute made useful things from plants?

5. What are the names of some black doctors and what did they do to save lives?

6. Who are some black people in sports?

7. What are the names of some black Americans who help make the laws?

8. When did Afro-Americans start fighting for their right to vote and to enjoy all of the freedoms of other Americans?

9. What did Mrs. Rosa Parks do?

People To Remember

You have read about many famous black people in this book. Some of them did things that helped other people. Some of them only led lives that were different from other people. Choose one of the people you have read about and on a separate sheet of paper tell why you enjoyed their story best.

Things for Hard Workers To Do

1. Act out the story of Mrs. Rosa Parks refusing to give up her seat on the bus.

2. Listen to records of famous black musicians.

3. Invite outstanding black people from your city to visit your school.

4. Learn some of Langston Hughes' and Gwendolyn Brooks' poems.

5. Learn the names of schools and streets in your city that are named after famous black people.

6. Talk about how each boy and girl in America can help make it a better place in their homes, schools, churches, and neighborhoods. How is your school doing these things?

Other Famous Afro-Americans

The black, red, yellow, and white skinned man has always shared this world. Each group has a special place in the story of man. It is only in the last few years that man has begun to know how important it is to get along together in this world we share. This book has told you something about the black man and his problems in this world. Below are some more famous black people mentioned in the book whom you may want to learn more about in your library.

Sojourner Truth (1797-1885) A slave who became the first black to speak against slavery.*

Booker T. Washington (1856-1915) The founder and President of Tuskegee Institute, a college for blacks.

Louis Armstrong (1900-   ) A cornet player who has been sent on three world tours as a goodwill ambassador by the United States.*

Estevanico (?) A man who helped explore Arizona and New Mexico with the Spanish in 1527*

138

Paul Laurence Dunbar (1872-1906) A poet who wrote many of his poems in the language of the slaves. He wrote many stories for boys and girls.*

Dr. Theodore K. Lawless (1892-   ) A doctor in Chicago, Illinois who has helped in finding ways to better treat leprosy, a terrible skin disease.*

Dr. George Washington Carver (1864-1943) A scientist who found new ways to use the peanut, soybean, and the sweet potato.*

Joe Louis (1914-   ) A prize fighter who held the heavyweight championship for 22 years.*

Adam Clayton Powell, Sr. (1865-1953) Built the Abyssinian Baptist Church of New York into the world's largest black congregation.

Marian Anderson (1902-   ) Thought to be the finest black woman singer. She was the first black to sing at the Metropolitan Opera.*

*These people have been mentioned in the unit pages of this book.

Vocabulary

The words used in this book should be familiar to students reading at third grade level. For those students reading at third grade level, a greater understanding of the subject matter will result if special emphasis is placed on the following words or phrases. The numbers indicate the page on which the word or phrase first appears.

Commentary for Teachers

Afro-Americans, Then and Now is basically an adaptation of Afro-American history for children in the primary grades, but because of high interest level it may serve older children as well.

At this writing, the controversy over African and Afro-American history is so intense as to force us to re-examine the structure, content, and purpose of history. In this context, it is well to start with the etymology of the word, history. History, in many western languages, can be easily traced to the Greek word, *istorie*, which meant inquiry. Early Greek historians were called logographers and their function was to study the world around them or, in a word, life. Eventually, the word history began to encompass not only the inquiry or statement of life's events but also the events, themselves. This double connotation of history is extremely important to our discussion. For, in French, the word history also carries the meaning of judging. Inherent in the process of recording events, is a value judgment of what to record and how to record it. Hence, the word story (which owes its origin to the same Greek word as history) may be a more appropriate designation for the recording of life's events than history. In other words, we are raising the question as to whether the term history should refer only to life's events and the term story be used to refer to the record of life's events.

In the light of this distinction, Afro-American history, though virtually unrecorded, is as real as any recorded ethnic history. But it is the Afro-American story that has been distorted.

Increasing numbers of black historians insist that, since the bulk of Afro-American history has been researched and recorded within the European framework, vital heroes, issues and elements in the black experience have been neglected. A great deal of interest is also evident in the oral tradition among black people here and in Africa. Teachers at the primary grades may begin to suggest research projects that explore the oral tradition. Children may ask about their family trees by questioning relatives and find out about historical figures and events by interviewing neighbors, friends, and other resource people such as ministers, social workers, and businessmen. They need to begin also to understand the dynamics of the historic era of today. What are the forces and institutions which affect their destiny? Who owns the local supermarkets? How do these businesses affect national politics and economics? Who are their favorite entertainers and athletes? How do they become famous? Who makes the laws?

Nearly as important as its content and its special relevancy to black children is the potential of this book for multi-disciplinary instruction. Because we view history as the phenomena of life and necessarily touching bases with all disciplines, there is ample opportunity to include art, music, creative dramatics, geography, language arts, and simple research methods while introducing the children to history. The prescribed activities are intended only to suggest to the teacher novel and interesting techniques in making history a viable and stimulating subject. There are also many opportunities to stimulate critical thinking on the part of the students. Hence, nothing that is suggested herein is intended to dictate or to encroach upon the role of the teacher, but rather to serve as a point of departure for the teacher to use his or her own creativity.

Fundamental to the instruction of Afro-American history is the teacher's own attitudes toward black children and the black community. If the teacher is narrow, negative, naive, or patronizing, then the text will be ineffective. On the other hand, if the teacher is open, inquiring, knowledgeable about the black community, respects the dignity and self-determination of black people, and understands their unique historical plight, then the text will serve its designated purpose.

The fact that children are daily at the mercy of television underscores the need for a realistic approach to history. Too long have we underestimated the child's tolerance for reality. Poor, black children have been especially victimized by our naive assessment of their strengths. By denying reality, whether in history, current events, literature, or any other subjects, we are actually misrepresenting the facts. Thus, History as well as the total curriculum must be reality-based.

The absence of a serious inquiry into history at the primary level may be the chief contributing factor to the heightened identity-crisis of America's youth. Thus, Afro-Americans, Then and Now is an effort to give the child a sense of identity, an understanding of his relationship to the past, present, and future, and a guide to his role as a self-determining agent.

Afro-Americans have made major contributions in all fields of human endeavor. Listed below are some additional contemporary Afro-Americans who have made outstanding contributions in their fields. You may wish to use their brief biographies as supplementary or enrichment material for this text.

Clarence Larry—Inventor of an instrument called a recording retinoscope stereoscope that can take still

142

or moving pictures of an astronaut's eyes during a simulated space flight.

Leontyne Price—Native of Mississippi. Concert and opera singer. Has performed in every major opera house in the world.

Theodore K. Lawless—(1892-   ). Leading skin specialist—works in Chicago. Educated at Talledega, University of Kansas, Columbia, Harvard, and M.D. from Northwestern. Worked abroad. Made contributions in the scientific treatment of leprosy.

Ulysses Kay—(1917-   ). Born in Tucson, Arizona on January 7th. Graduate of University of Arizona in 1938. Mus. M. from Eastman School of Music in 1940. Studied at Yale 1941-42. Studied at Columbia 1946-48. Alice M. Ditson Fellow 1946-47. Rosenwald Fellow 1947-49. Composed and conducted music for film, "The Quiet One", in 1948. First published works were performed by Rochester Civic Orchestra under Howard Hanson. Composed "Suite for Orchestra" and Solemn Prelude".

Juanita Kidd Stout—(1919-   ). Born in Wewoka, Oklahoma, on March 17th. Admitted to D.C. Bar in 1950. Pennsylvania Bar in 1954. Taught music in elementary school, 1930-41. First elected Negro woman judge, 1959-62. Judge of County Court in Philadelphia 1962---.

For background you may want to read some of the books used in the preparation of this text.

Bennett, Lerone. *Before the Mayflower*. Johnson Pub. Co., Chicago, 1966

Bontempts, Arna. *100 Years of Negro Freedom*. Dodd, Mead and Co., New York, 1965.

Bontempts, Arna. *The Story of the Negro*.

Davidson, Basil. *A Guide to African History*. Doubleday and Co., Inc., Garden City, N.Y. 1965.

Davidson, Basil. *Black Mother*, Little, Brown and Co., Boston, 1961

Davidson, Basil. *The African Past*. Little, Brown and Co., Boston, 1964.

Du Bois, W. E. Burghart. *The Souls of Black Folk*. Fawcett Pub. Inc., 1961.

Franklin, John Hope. *Reconstruction After the Civil War.* University of Chicago Press, 1966.

Hughes, Langston. *An African Treasury.* Crown Publishers, Inc., 1960.

Hughes, Langston. *The First Book of Africa.* Franklin Watts, Inc., N.Y. 1960.

Katz, William. *Eyewitness: The Negro in American History.* Pitman Publishing Corporation, N.Y., 1967.

Life Magazine Editors. *I Have A Dream, The Story of Martin Luther King in Text and Pictures.* Time-Life Books, N.Y., 1968.

Patterson, Lillie, *Frederick Douglass.* Dell Publishing Co., Inc., N.Y., 1965.

Patrick, John J. *The Progress of the Afro-American.* Benefic Press, Westchester, Illinois, 1969.

Rose, Arnold, *The Negro in America.* Harper and Row, N.Y., 1964

Quarles, Benjamin. *The Negro in the Making of America.* Macmillan Co., N.Y., 1964.

Stratton, Madeline. *Negroes Who Helped Build America.* Ginn and Co., Boston, 1965.

Toppin, Edgar. *A Mark Well Made.* Rand McNally and Co., Chicago, 1967.

Wish, Harvey. *The Negro Since Emancipation.* Prentice Hall, Inc., 1964.

ACKNOWLEDGEMENTS

Our thanks to the following for permission to reproduce the art and photographs that appear on the pages indicated:

Bettman Archive, 35, 46, 69

Culver Pictures, Inc., 52, 56, 66, 86

Davis, Michael, 34, 70

Ebony-Johnson Publishing Company, 112

Explorer's Club, 74

Historical Pictures Service, 27, 44, 48, 96

Kedzie, Thomas, title page

Ranft, Max, 21, 39, 43, 47, 51, 55, 59, 77, 81, 85, 89, 93, 107, 111, 115, 119, 123, 127, 131, 135

Teason, James, 6, 12-13, 18, 24, 28-29, 33, 36, 40, 62, 78, 100-101

United Press International, 14, 17, 72, 82, 90, 102, 104, 108, 116, 120, 124, 128, 132

Editors, Louisa M. Johnston, Betty J. Shangle

Kenneth Lattimore —
Morty Lattimore —
Gregory Lattimore —
Andre Lattimore —